'Til Stress Do Us Part

A Guide to Modern Love by Reverend Will B. Dunn

DOUG MARLETTE

Longstreet Press
Atlanta, Georgia

For Melinda, with love

Published by
LONGSTREET PRESS, INC.
2150 Newmarket Parkway
Suite 102
Marietta, Georgia 30067

Copyright © 1989 by Doug Marlette

Kudzu is syndicated by Creators Syndicate, Los Angeles,
California.

Printed in the United States of America

1st printing, 1989

Library of Congress Catalog Number 88-083936

ISBN 0-929264-15-0

This book was printed by Arcata Graphics/Kingsport
in Kingsport, Tennessee.

Cover design by Paulette Lambert. Front cover photo by
Floyd Jillson. Back cover photo by Mark B. Sluder.

Yuppie Love

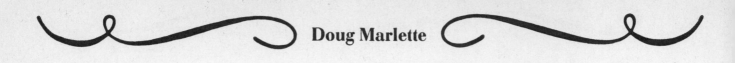

Doug Marlette

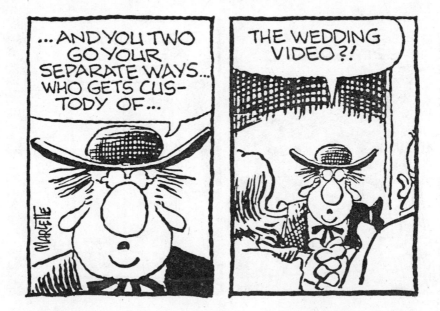

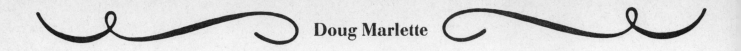

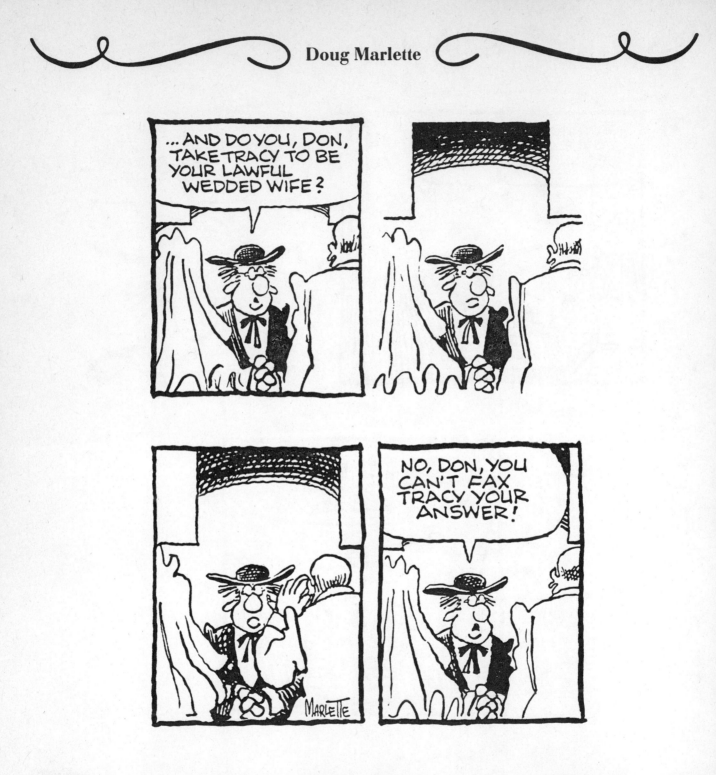

The Vow Thing

33

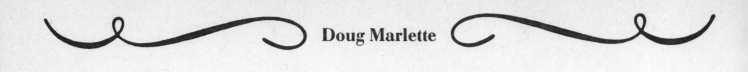

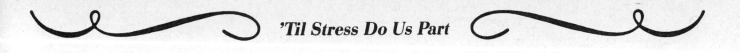

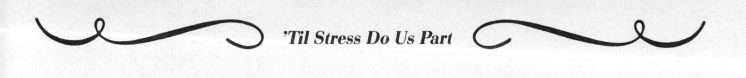

Doug Marlette

63

For Better
or the Pits

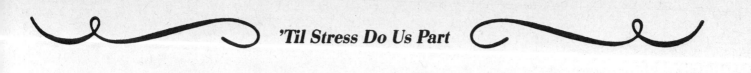

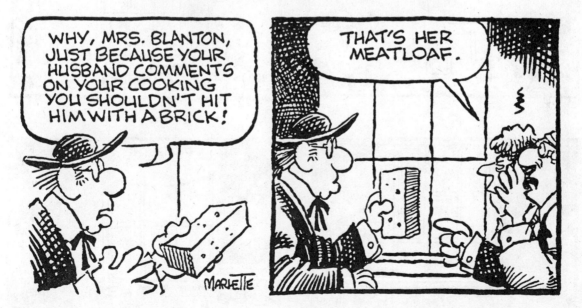

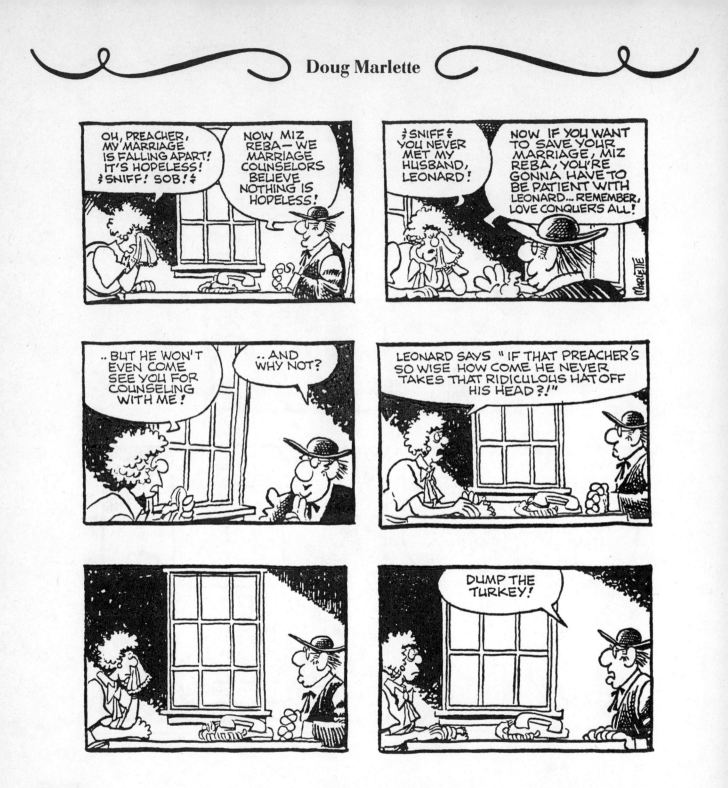

77

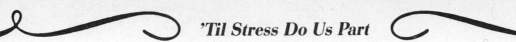

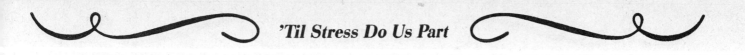

Irreconcilable Differences

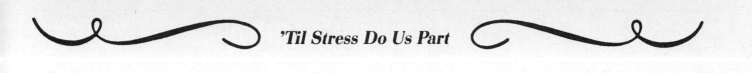

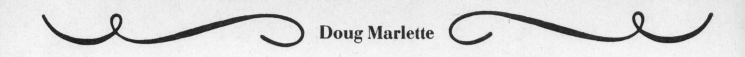

101

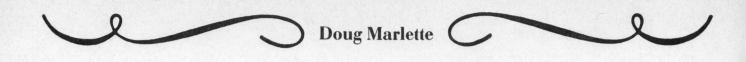

103

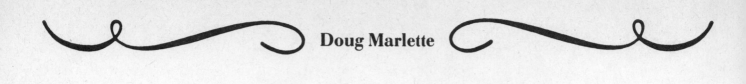

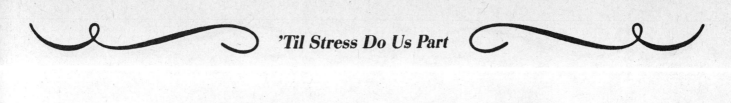

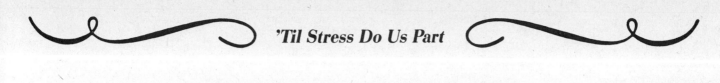

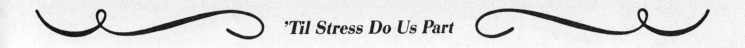

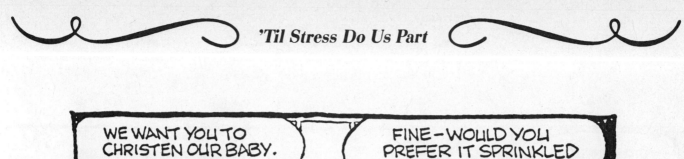

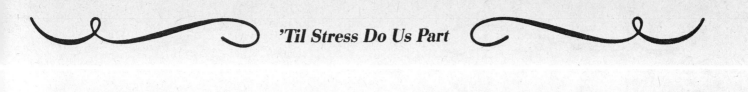

125